The Germans

Narratives of American Families

By

Bonnie S. Johnston

Copyright 2016

\2

\3

THE GERMANS
By Bonnie S. Johnston

Copyright 2016

Other works by Bonnie S. Johnston

Historical Novels

THE DARK SIDE OF THE MOUNTAIN
THE DARK SIDE OF THE TRAIL
THE DARK SIDE OF THE RIVER

Narratives

SALEM FAMILIES
THE ROAD FROM JAMESTOWN
THE ENGLISH SEAMAN AND HIS
REMARKABLE WIFE

\4

Author's Notes

During the eighteenth century, thousands of German families left war-torn Europe and made the treacherous voyage to America. For the most part, they succeeded and left tens of thousands of descendants who inherited their qualities of hard work and perseverance.

This narrative tells the stories of four of these families: the Bushes, Mallows, Riffles and Lamberts. The information related is based on records, family stories that vary greatly, and historical research, but is not meant to be a source for proven genealogical descent. Instead, this work combines a variety of sources to tell the stories of remarkable people who endured endless hardship and loss during the settling of America. Perhaps a few readers will discover their ancestors and hints for further research.

The Riffles, in particular, cause much confusion in the research of the family. George Strunk Riffle, the grandson of the immigrant Jacob, has a very colorful history as related in this narrative. His descendants may be distressed at the information provided, but may consult the Montgomery County, Ohio, records to find information about his stay in Ohio. There is no proof that his middle name Strunk was his mother's maiden name, but it seems highly probable.

These Germans came to the colony of Pennsylvania before 1750 and settled in what is now Berks County. Within a few years most of them were enticed by land speculators to move to the frontier of Virginia where they were confronted by the French and Indian War, an event they could not have imagined. Their lives were affected by the Native Americans who fought to keep their ancestral land and culture. Family members were killed and some taken captive during this time; however, others joined militia groups, fought the Indians and, eventually, the British during the American Revolution .The Native Americans never regained their lands or their culture, and their stories have faded into the dust bin of history.

The Germans

During the first half of the eighteenth century many Germans living under severe repression immigrated to America. They brought large families, the Lutheran faith, and the German language and culture. The colony of Pennsylvania, founded in 1681 by William Penn, offered opportunity for many poor Europeans. Germans, in particular, came in droves during the eighteenth century.

The voyage was not easy for these determined Germans. When the overloaded ships landed at Philadelphia, passengers were required to remain on board until their passages were paid in full. Those who could not pay were "purchased" for a period of years or indentured their children to wealthy families who waited for the opportunity for cheap labor.

In 1750, Gottlieb Mittelberger, a German immigrant who did not like America, wrote of his voyage and the process. (Jamestown.org)

The sale of human beings in the market on board the ship is carried on. . . Every day. . . High born Germans bargain how long they will have to serve for their passage money. . . Many parents must sell and trade away their children . . . children above ten years can take part of their parents' debt upon themselves.

Work and labor in this new and wild land are very hard and manifold, and many a one who came there in his old age must work very hard to his end. . . Work mostly consists in cutting wood, felling oak trees, rooting out . . . clearing large tracts of forests. Such forests, being cleared are then laid out for fields and meadows.

In this hot land, they fully experience what God has imposed upon man for his Sin and disobedience . . . let him do so in his own country, and not in America for he will not fare better in America. . . {emigrants} are very foolish if they believe that roasted pigeons will fly into their mouths in America or Pennsylvania without their working for them. How miserably and wretchedly so many thousands German families have forced since they lost all their cash means in consequence of the long and tedious journey because many of them died miserably and were thrown into the water. . .

These Germans as described in this narrative had not read Mittelberger's assessment of the New World, and, if they had, would not have been deterred. After all, they were escaping war-torn Europe where their lives were intolerable. They would come to America, and most would persevere despite the miserable voyage and the difficult labor. Some were forced to indenture their children, but hope for success always loomed on the horizon.

Bush

The Germans proved to be industrious farmers and left their marks in the colonies. One of these families was the Bush family who eventually settled in a dangerous area on the frontier of Virginia during the period of the border wars with the French and Indians. It should be noted that there were many other Bush families who immigrated at different times.

After a long trip from Germany, Hans Michael Bush and wife Maria Eva Plattner, daughter of Michael Plattner and Maria Catherina Reichard of Baden, arrived in Philadelphia on 1733 on the ship *Hope*. The couple brought their children including Johann Ludwig (Lewis) age 11, George Adam, age 13, Maria, age 9, and Johannes Michael, age 7. Three younger children, ages 5, 3, and 4 months, were either left behind in Germany to come later or actually made the trip and died during the voyage or shortly after arrival. It seems unlikely that such young children were left behind however, but no records exist to explain their fates.

In those days, a tax was required of those who left Germany. This tax is recorded in the Manumission Papers, Karisruhe Archives, located in Germany. Both Hans Michael and wife Eva were reportedly born in Zuzanhausen, Daisbach, where their children were baptized according to these records.

The Bush family settled in Berks County, Pennsylvania, along with other German families in the Tulpehocken area. Hans Michael claimed land and farmed for sixteen years. His children spoke German and attended the Lutheran Church. Illiteracy was very common, but the Lutheran Church promoted literacy, and the Bushes probably spoke English and wrote English to some extent.

Reportedly, Hans Michael died in 1749 and was buried on his own land, a common practice at that time. There had been no Indian trouble during these years. It was yet to come.

The second son of Hans Michael and Eva Bush, Lewis, was twenty-six when his father died in 1749. He had spent sixteen years in the Tulpehocken Valley and had married there. For at least another year, Lewis and his brothers, George Adam, and Johannes Michael, remained in Pennsylvania, presumably farming the land their father had claimed and left them.

Around 1744 Lewis married Eva Hyer, whose family emigrated from Switzerland on the ship *Grace* in 1737 when she was nine years old. The Hyers (Heier) were Swiss Protestants who sought freedom of religion. The Hyers, Leonard and Clara Lutzler, had also settled in the Tulpehocken Valley.

By 1750, Michael and Eva's sons had sold their land and made their way to the frontier of Virginia. They may have been enticed by unscrupulous land speculators who promised much and delivered little. Leonard, Eva's father, was listed as living in Augusta County, Virginia by 1750, the area where the Bushes settled. It is likely that the younger Bushes followed Hyer to the frontier.

When the Germans settled in Virginia during this time, the claiming of vacant land was accomplished by several means. Building a cabin and growing a crop of grain entitled a man to four hundred acres. The "cabin right" gave a family a claim of forty acres if they built a log hut on a certain tract.

For some years the woods supplied these early settlers with their subsistence. It was not uncommon for families to live several months without a mouthful of bread. Breakfast was often obtained from the woods. Fur constituted money, for settlers had nothing else to give in exchange for rifles, salt, and other supplies.

Frontier life was extremely difficult and primitive. Initial cabins were largely one room containing one large fireplace where all the cooking was done. Diet consisted of wild game and corn pone with few vegetables. Roads were poor, and all white males above the age of sixteen, except ferrymen and owners of two or more slaves, were required to work on them. Clothing was entirely homemade, and ornaments such as buckles were practically nonexistent. Men protected their families and provided food while women bore children, took care of them, and performed endless household chores. Social gatherings were very few, but weddings provided the best opportunity for social gatherings.

Lewis and Eva, as did most early immigrants, produced a child every two years and had eight, including Michael, number four, born in 1750, probably in Augusta County, Virginia. The Bushes, Hyers, and others appear in the South branch area of Augusta County in the early 1750s.

Lewis' brother Michael accompanied him to the South Branch Valley while older brother George Adam moved further west to the next valley. Eva, the widow, resided with son Michael who remained in Augusta County the rest of his life.

Imagine a one room cabin, lighted only by a fire burning in a large, open fireplace, flickering light illuminating the faces of those who sought its warmth. Smells of ashes and cooked food permeate the small room as the wife sits in a chair, knitting and mending for her brood of many children, baby asleep in a wooden cradle, another in a trundle bed and several in the cold loft above her. The father sits on a stool as he patiently cleans his musket while the only sounds surrounding them are the crackle of the fire and the howling wind blowing outside. Both husband and wife are silent, eyes tired and sleep deprived.

While his family remained in their primitive cabin on the frontier, Lewis Bush joined the militia and fought with the Augusta troops during Dunmore's War in 1774. He and son Michael probably fought at the battle of Point Pleasant, but records are incomplete or nonexistent. Years later in 1799, Lewis, wife Eva, and their children moved to Ohio, Ross County. It is difficult to imagine Lewis and Eva, close to seventy years old, making such a move. Lewis died in 1802 and Eva in 1813. Both are buried in Ross County, Ohio, where their descendants live to this day.

Virginia was a dangerous place when the Bushes arrived in the 1750s. The French and Indian War, which had simmered for years, erupted in 1754, and Indian raids upon the settlers commenced all along the frontier. In 1758 the Indians destroyed two forts in Augusta County: Ft. Seybert and the Upper Tract Fort. Other forts were burned, hundreds of whites taken captive, and settlers scalped.

Despite difficult times, Michael and Eva's grandsons proved to be ambitious and daring. John Bush, George Adam's son, is remembered today as a fearless frontiersman.

His brothers were also frontiersmen who rode with General Clark into both Ohio and Kentucky during this time.

Virginia contains several beautiful valleys including the Tygart Valley where, in 1762, two deserters from Ft. Pitt, the Pringle brothers, settled in a large sycamore tree. The old tree allowed a hollowed, protective area where people actually could reside. Several other families joined them off and on, including the Riffles, another German family discussed in this narrative.

It is almost impossible to imagine living in a tree today. Sycamore trees were abundant in Virginia and grew to be quite large. An old tree might very well have had a rotten center, allowing enterprising men to hack out an opening ten or more feet in diameter. They would be spared the labor of building a cabin and were provided with substantial shelter. It is even harder to imagine the lives of the Pringle wives, burdened with children and forced to live in a tree.

Around 1765, the Pringle brothers were forced to leave the safety of their tree because of lack of supplies, and they made the trip east to Augusta County settlements. By 1770, after discovering that they were no longer in military danger, one of the brothers returned with his family and others, including John Bush, for settlement.

Eventually building a cabin, Bush made a claim for two hundred acres of land in 1771, but his claim was not official until ten years later when claims for unpatented lands were finally settled.

Along with Michael, Lewis and Leonard Bush, John Bush also fought at the battle of Pt. Pleasant during Dunmore's War in 1774 and was listed on the payroll of John Robertson's Company in the Pittsburgh Pay Rolls in 1775.

Around that time John Bush is credited with building a fort which allowed protection for the settlers until 1782 when it was burned by the Indians. The fort was located along the Buckhannon River, the exact location no longer known. Bush had married Mary Hacker around 1774 in that area where her family were early settlers.

Although the French and Indian War ended by 1759, the Indians were not appeased, and by 1770 had resumed their raids against the settlers on the frontier who paid no attention to treaties and continued to move west.

In 1782 John Bush was listed on the tax list of Hampshire County near the Buckhannon River. However, residents of the Buckhannon River Valley left in fear when Bush's Fort fell that year to the Indians. Varying accounts of Bush's escapades at that time have been passed down.

When the fort fell, Bush and two others escaped and rode back to the Tygart Valley for safety. The Indian raiding party chased the men, but Bush managed to get away while the others were killed.

The Indian forces were led by Leonard Schoolcraft, a Tory, who had a vendetta against Bush for some reason. Although Bush made it safely to the Tygart Valley, the Indian forces followed. A few days later Bush and his wife were following two men on horseback when the Indians attacked again. The Bushes escaped on one of the horses when the two men with them were killed. It did not bode well for anyone who accompanied John Bush it seemed.

Eventually, by the middle 1780s, Bush and family moved back to the Buckhannon River Valley and were listed on tax lists there. They no doubt thought the Indian threat had dissipated at that time. However, the Shawnee and Delaware were keeping very busy as they raided the Kentucky settlements and killed as many settlers as they could along the Ohio River. It was only a matter of time until some of the raiding parties would venture farther into Virginia.

In the meantime, Bush's father, George Adam, who had come to America at age thirteen with his father, made a pioneer settlement on Freeman's Creek in nearby Lewis County and offered to trade a piece of his land for John's land on the Buckhannon River. So John moved to Freeman's Creek in 1790, lived with his father for a period as he completed his cabin. Soon the family moved into the new structure. It is not recorded how Mary Bush felt about all of these moves and the danger that surrounded her.

On April 24, 1791, almost a decade after Bush was almost killed by the Indians twice, he sent two of his children out to drive cattle. Soon Bush heard screams and went to the cabin door. He was met by several Indians who shot him. Mary Bush assisted her husband and reportedly killed five Indians with an ax and pulled John back into the cabin. She held the door while the Indians shot twenty bullets through it. Amazingly, she lived, and the story of her bravery became part of history. It is probable that the story has been exaggerated over the years; however, even if there were only two Indians and five shots, Mary's heroism is apparent.

One of the Indians who shot Bush was none other than Leonard Schoolcraft, a renegade white who had been captured by the Indians years before. Schoolcraft had taken an Indian wife, a Miss Nyssander, thought to be the daughter of chief Killbuck, the well-known leader of many raids during the previous decade. Tradition records that Schoolcraft's voice was heard by Bush's wife while she was protecting her husband. During the attempted massacre, Adam Bush, John's brother, came to investigate but failed to save the two Bush children.

Within two weeks John Bush died of his wounds. He had asked his father George to deed over the promised land to his wife. Old George never got around to doing so and evidently sold the land, perhaps more than once. The widow and children recovered the land years after John died but had to go to court to do so. George reportedly was a heavy drinker and involved in unscrupulous land deals. He may have lived to be one hundred years old in the depths of alcoholism and senility. He saw John's widow as a witch and never made good on his promise.

It is not known why Schoolcraft had such hate for John Bush. In the previous decade thirteen members Schoolcraft's family had been killed or captured by the Indians including Schoolcraft himself. Some believe that he had loved Mary West of the Buckhannon area but she refused him and married another. He participated in the West massacre when Mary West was killed and scalped. John Bush's connection was unclear, but he may have been a friend of the Wests. Bush's two captured children were thought to have been returned in two years, one then dying and the other running off with a Canadian fiancé and never heard from again.

Five of Schoolcraft's children and his wife were later killed by a Shawnee raiding party, but several Schoolcraft children lived and left descendants as did John and Mary Bush.

A son of Lewis and Eva, Michael Bush settled on "Bush's Run" near Shaver's Run in the Tygart Valley in 1768; Michael was an original settler of Petty's Fort tract, Valley Bend, according to the Augusta County land commission. In 1788, Bush was listed on Robert Harrison's company in the Rockingham Militia along with father Lewis. Lewis was listed with one horse, Michael with five horses and brother Leonard with six horses, suggesting that the Bushes had fared well. That same year Michael and Leonard Bush laid out a road, the responsibility of those who lived in the area.

Ten years later, Michael and wife moved to Ohio where they remained until their deaths. Michael is listed as a Revolutionary War Veteran buried in Fayette County, Ohio. He is listed as a private from Hardy County, Virginia, born in Frederick County 1750, married Magdalene, and died in Frankfort, Ohio, in 1825. He was buried near Austin in Concord Township. Michael's sister Sarah had married Adam Mallow and moved to Ohio with the rest of the Lewis Bush family. Michael died in 1825, and Magdalene had died earlier in 1821.

John Bush, perhaps named after his frontiersman uncle, a son of Michael and

Magdalena, was born in 1773 in what is now Pendleton County. In 1795 he married Mary Wise, a daughter of John Wise and Mary Heier, the later of who went to Ohio with her daughter Mary, the wife of John Bush. At her death at age sixty six, Bush placed Mary Wise's gravestone near his parents, Michael and Magdalene, a tribute to his opinion of his mother-in-law.

John outlived three wives according to the *The History of Fayette County* which states that Michael Bush, a son of Lewis Bush, fathered John Bush who married first Mary Wise of Hardy County, Virginia; second Kezia Schofield; and third Elizabeth Ross.

Another account of the Ohio Bushes can be found in *The History of_Ross County Ohio*.

In 1799, John and Michael Bush came from Virginia, and as soon as possible erected a mill and distillery near where the Union Church now stands. The water power proving insufficient, they soon made a new race and removed the mill to a point opposite the present Railroad station (1880) This was both a grist mill and saw mill . . . the Bushes had a general store for many years. This was probably the first mill in the present township. It is still standing and in operation . . . Mr. Solomon Bush, son of John Bush, the pioneer miller and merchant, says that an election was held at his father's house as early as the year 1800, and that elections were held continually there until . . . 1817.

In 1827 there was organized . . . a Union church, intended to be undenominational in its character. . . Adam Mallow, John and Solomon Bush were its first trustees . . . erected on the Frankfort and Herold's Creek . . . upon land donated by John Bush . . . occupied in 1828 . . . dunkards quite numerous.

John Bush and Mary Wise had the following children: Solomon, Elizabeth, Mary, Jacob, Jesse, John, Lavinia, Julia and William. All were born on the Bush farm in Ross County, Ohio. Mary died before 1827 when John married Kezia Scofield and had two more children before he married a third time. Remarkably, John lived to be ninety-five years old and died in 1868, outliving three wives.

William Bush, a son of John Bush, was born in 1813 in Ross County and married Nancy Mallow, his second cousin. The Mallows had come to Ross County in 1806 several years after the Bushes. Their relationship as second cousins stemmed from

William Bush's grandfather Michael's sister Sarah who had married Adam Mallow, Nancy's grandfather, in Virginia. Adam had been a captive of the Shawnee for over six years during the French and Indian War.

The families were well acquainted for several generations. William and Nancy had four children including John, Sarah, Mary Jane and Martha E. In the early 1880s William, Nancy and son William moved to Sedgwick County, Kansas. Both Nancy and William were over sixty years old and may have made the move by train in order to claim the newly opened area of Kansas. It is even possible they made the move by wagon. They had sold their farm in Ohio and disappeared until Find-a-Grave located their graves in the El Paso Cemetery in Kansas. Nancy died in 1891 and William in 1894. It is interesting that the couple left a large extended family and prosperity in Ohio to follow son William to Kansas. Kansas records are scarce so we cannot discern their motives, but they must have been moderately successful since William purchased a cemetery plot and descendants are buried there. Their other children remained in Ohio.

\26

Mallow

Another German family of note arrived sixteen years after the Bushes on the ship *Phoenix*, which docked in Philadelphia on September 15, 1749. Approximately five hundred and fifty Germans disembarked including brothers Johan Michael and Hans George Mallo. The family Mallo is recorded in Griesbach, Germany, for several hundred years. Michael's father was Hans Diebolt Mallo, born in 1681 and died in 1730. He married Anna Catherine Voltz, born in 1694, daughter of Hans Jacob Voltz. Records of the Mallo family go back even further in Griesbach. Upon disembarking the ship, Johan, called Michael, signed his name, unlike many who were signed in by a clerk. Michael was literate.

William Penn, head of the Pennsylvania Colony, induced thousands of Germans from the Rhine area of Germany to come to America. These Mallo brothers were emigrating because of religious persecution and terrible conditions in Germany. They were Lutherans and farmers. Michael was twenty nine years old at the time of his immigration and was accompanied by his pregnant wife Anna Margaretha whose surname is unknown.

Shortly, the Mallows settled in the Tulpehocken Valley in Pennsylvania which had been settled by German Lutherans in an adventurous and hazardous migration that occurred in the spring of 1723, when a group of fifteen German Palatine families left the Schoharie Valley of New York to settle in the Tulpehocken region of present Berks County. Soon, the Tulpehocken settlement became a thriving settlement. Mallows' daughter Anna Maria was born one month after their arrival and baptized in Christ Lutheran church in Stouchburg.

Less than three years later, Mallow sought the unsettled land of Virginia as did many other German families who were offered attractive prices for land by speculators. Settlement in the remote wilderness in a time of peace was difficult, but settling during a time of potential Indian attacks took extreme endurance. In 1753, the couple crossed the mountains and settled on South Fork Mountain by the South Branch of the Potomac.

It is difficult to imagine the hardship of a trip over one hundred and fifty miles without lodging or much protection during inclement weather. Roads were rough and pitted with rocks and obstructions but packed hard from use. During wet weather wagon wheels stuck in the mud and often caused numerous delays.

Women and children sat on hard wood seats and felt every bump in the road. Older children and the father walked with sticks prodding livestock or rode horses next to the wagons. Food was procured along the way by hunting or bartering with other settlers who had settled along the what was called "The Great Migration Road". At this time, however, many cabins were empty, their residents having moved east to safety during the French and Indian War.

By 1757, about forty families were living in the South Branch area of Virginia. The Germans began to arrive in 1748 when the area was primarily forest with only a few clearings near the water courses. A few, brave Scots-Irish had settled there even earlier. These earlier settlers had claimed the best land, the bottoms which lay by the river. There was no going back for those who braved settlement. Their land had been sold, and a trip back to Pennsylvania was next to impossible.

When the Mallows moved to the settlement in Augusta County, there were no schools. However, school training was not entirely forgotten. Teaching in those days was considered a private, not a public, matter, and to a large extent was conducted through the German Lutheran church in the German tongue. Otherwise, with German-speaking as well as English-speaking settlers, the only education provided was through tutoring by parents who were competent to teach their own children. Illiteracy was predominant, and women were more illiterate than men. Some of the more prominent settlers could sign their names only by means of a mark.

By the time the Mallows reached the South Branch area, the Mallows had added to their family son Adam, born October 6, 1751, followed by three others, including a baby daughter called Sarah. Mallow settled on land that adjoined Jacob Seybert's, both families having emigrated from the German area in Pennsylvania, Seybert having arrived in 1749. Mallow might have been disappointed in his claim since it did not contain bottom lands and lay on the side of a mountain, but the family could not move back to Pennsylvania.

Western Virginia had become a dangerous place to live at this period, as numerous raids had been made on the frontier by the Shawnee and Delaware Indians under the well-known and ferocious chief, Killbuck. Their cruelty was encouraged by the French, who promised rewards for scalps, as well as restoration of their land. They were fighting for their land and culture.

By 1750 both the English and the French claimed the territory along the Ohio and Mississippi Rivers. Both countries mounted military efforts to secure these lands, which, in fact, belonged to the American Indians. The Indians united with the French and defeated English General Braddock in 1753 in western Pennsylvania. However, nothing was truly settled, and the Indians continued their vicious attacks on the white settlers who inhabited the frontiers of Virginia and Pennsylvania and what would become Kentucky. Although these German settlers were well suited for the frontier life and were industrious and, for the most part, successful, they were not prepared for the French and Indian War during which one thousand Virginians were killed.

The plan was for France to take possession of the British area of North America and for France and her allies to divide the colonies among themselves. When the English government granted privileges beyond the Allegheny Mountains to the Virginia Ohio Company, the French increased their efforts to establish a chain of forts from Canada to their Mississippi settlements. The objective was to confine the English colonies to the Atlantic coast. The French had a long-standing treaty with the Iroquois Indians, and the Iroquois were greatly feared by every other Indian tribe in the whole area including the Shawnees and the Delawares.

During the years 1755 through 1758, the Shawnees, along with other tribes and the French, attacked many British settlements in Virginia, Maryland, and Pennsylvania. Many settlers were killed and others taken captive. Farms and crops were destroyed. Indians attacked at will and plundered and murdered many entire families.

During these years, many atrocities occurred on both sides of the conflict. Children and women were taken into captivity; men were brutally shot and scalped. The French openly encouraged the Indians to attack and kill all English settlers. The Delawares and Shawnees allied with the French, controlled the forests and were able to take captives long distances, including to the Ohio and the Mississippi River areas. Despite being plucked from their white families, many returned captives retained longings for their Indian life styles and the lands to which they had been taken. The Indians encouraged their captives to integrate into Indian life. In most cases these captives were treated well.

In January 1756, Colonel George Washington recommended to Virginia Governor Dinwiddie that a series of forts be constructed along the mountains, two of them high up on the South Branch of the Potomac. Construction began that fall. In March of 1757, Jacob Seybert was commissioned a Captain to head up the militia on the South Branch of which Michael Mallow was a part. Records have been preserved showing Mallow's scouting activities, muster rolls, and requisitions of this Augusta County Militia.

During this time Chief Killbuck led the Shawnees and Delawares and others in a "Death Claim" for all the land near the Blue

Ridge Mountains and the Ohio River. These Indians were fighting for their homelands. In 1755 and 1756 the "old Indian Chief Killbuck" came across the Allegheny Mountains and attacked the settlers of Patterson's Creek Valley, Virginia. Historical accounts describe Chief Killbuck as cunning, ferocious, vengeful, and ugly. His name was associated with many Indian raids during the years 1753 through 1758.

Evidence is scarce, but it is thought Killbuck was born around 1719 in the Lehigh River area of Pennsylvania. His sister was the wife of the famous Delaware chief Netawatwees, Newcomer in English. As the English settlers began to move westward, Killbuck's Delaware clan moved to the Ohio country. During the French and Indian War, Killbuck became known as John Killbuck, Sr. or Bemino. He was also a medicine man and, by the French and Indian War, a war chief of the Delaware Turkey clan.

The first Augusta County attack occurred in June of 1756 when the Indians suddenly appeared and committed deliberate murder when they crept up behind a fence of a German farmer and shot him as he was ploughing. The settler tried to defend himself but was unable to do so. The Indians cut his head and scalped him; his wife and child were taken captive. After consuming all of the brandy they found, the Indians continued their raid by killing a neighbor child about four years old. Others were killed during that year and raids continued in 1757.

In 1758 according to one source, "a most severe blow now befell the weakened settlements of Augusta". The defense of Fort Upper Tract was entrusted to Capt. James Dunlap, who had commanded a detachment in the Big Sandy expedition earlier. This stockade along with Fort Seybert had been erected for the protection of the families who lived in the area. On April 27, this stockade was destroyed by Indians under the leadership of Chief Killbuck.

The local militia around Fort Seybert was away from home on a military expedition or securing supplies because there had been reports of up to sixteen men and boys killed in the area. It is unclear why these local men decided to make a trip of days, leaving their families in Fort Seybert. It may have been simply a matter of necessity to secure ammunition and supplies. Regardless, they chose a bad time to leave their wives and children.

A band of perhaps one Frenchman and fifty or sixty Indians appeared in the valley, and on April 27 captured and burned the Upper Tract fort killing twenty-two persons, including two young couples who had sought safety. The Indians then moved on to Ft. Seybert nine miles away.

The tragedy at Fort Seybert took place on the following day. The people slain in the massacre numbered seventeen, some accounts putting the number at twenty one or even more. There were at least twenty captives; accounts vary. Ft. Seybert, a larger stockade with a blockhouse, was situated on the South Fork River. It is probable that nearly sixty settlers lost their lives in these two attacks, but the some of the victims may have not been identified, and their mass grave on private property has never been exhumed.

One account states that early on that foggy morning, the War Chief Killbuck used the fog as cover to attack Fort Seybert, having destroyed Fort Upper Tract the day before. William Dyer, a resident of the fort, was out hunting when the Indians discovered and killed him. His sister Sarah Dyer Hawes, a young widow, was captured outside the fort along with her indentured servant called Wallace, both of whom had evidently decided to remain in the Hawes' cabin.

The length of the Indians' siege of this fort might have been as long as two days although the records vary. At any rate Captain Seybert's fifteen year old son Nicholas made attempts to defend the fort and its inhabitants. He spied an Indian, took aim, and shot and killed a warrior. Soon Killbuck changed his strategy and called to Captain Seybert to surrender in order to spare the residents of the fort. If not, his warriors would kill them all.

Seybert's son Nicholas and several others adamantly objected to a surrender, but Seybert did not listen. He was aware that only five men defended the fort and ammunition was low. When the gate was opened, Nicholas aimed at Killbuck, but the gun was knocked aside by his father or a man called Robertson. The bullet hit the ground. Killbuck's greeting to Captain Seybert was a strike on the mouth loosening several teeth. Nicholas continued to fight but was overcome.

Robertson, who evidently had sought safety within the fort, and possibly five or more women and children managed to escape during the confusion. Two or three people died in the fort fire including Jacob Seybert's mother Hannah Lawrence whose husband Henry had been killed by the Indians a year earlier, and George Moser, who had been wounded days earlier and brought to the fort for safety. Killbuck and his followers took money and supplies and the remaining settlers, mostly children, captive including six Seybert and five Mallow children.

Several reports explain that the entire group of Indians and captives traveled about one quarter of a mile from the destroyed fort. At that time the captives were divided into two groups, one with those whose lives would be spared, and another with those who would be killed. At Killbuck's signal, those on one log were brutally tomahawked and scalped while the remaining group was spared to march with the Indians back to the Ohio Territory.

Killbuck, as did most Indians, admired courage and bravery and desired to incorporate those individuals into his clan. He also preferred brunettes because they more closely resembled his people. The weak, the infirm, and the old were not tolerated. In particular, young children were liabilities on the nine day trip back to the Ohio River.

Michael Mallow's wife Anna Margaretha Mallow and their five children including nine year old Anna Maria, called Mary, Adam, baby Sarah and two unnamed sons had sought safety at Fort Seybert while Mallow and other local men left for supplies. The six were captured and marched with the others up the mountain to the site of the logs where they survived the slaughter.

The records of the three youngest Mallow children are non-existent except for Mallow's 1765 reference to five children taken at Fort Seybert. Several stories tell of the death of the baby, but the two little boys' deaths are not recorded, but they may have died on the trip or in Indian villages. The story of the death of the youngest Mallow daughter is related as follows.

Stories relate that on the first night the Indians and their captives camped at the big spring near what is now Kline, West Virginia. Anna Mallow was pregnant and carried her small daughter. At the Greenwalt Gap in this area the child cried. One of the warriors grabbed the baby and placed it on a rock forcing her mother to continue marching. He then bashed the child's head on the rock. Another report states that an infant cried along the march. The Indians were angry and killed the child and hung it in the forked branch of a dogwood tree.

The next morning, April 29, 1758, the group began their trip to the Ohio country. The Indians led the settlers along a trail through German Valley to the Ohio River, a nine day journey.

Another story explains that the Indians had collected settlers' valuables and carried them in an iron kettle. The burden became too heavy so the two Indians who carried this treasure eventually fell behind. They returned without the kettle, suggesting they had buried it on the trail. To this day people still seek the buried items which have never been found during the Treasure Mountain Festival, held annually at Franklin, West Virginia. One might wonder why the settlers brought valuable items to the fort if, indeed, they had any. It would have been more logical to bury such items on their property in hopes that the Indians would not discover them. The settlers no doubt left their livestock deep in the woods for the same reason. In any event, the settlers probably did not have wealth in terms of gold or silver but rather had tools which the Indians could use.

Another account states that, as the party was nearing the Ohio River, young defiant Nicholas Seybert remarked about a flock of turkeys flying high in the distance.

"You have sharp eyes," observed Killbuck. "Wasn't it you who killed our warrior?"

"Yes," replied the boy, "and I would have killed you if my gun hadn't been knocked down."

"You little devil," said the chief, "if you had killed me, my warriors would have given up and gone away. Brave boy, you'll make a good warrior. But don't tell my people what you did." (Rootsweb.com. March 2003).

Another story tells of another young man, James Dyer, age fourteen, who escaped and ran one half mile to the river. He was caught but spared because of his bravery and swiftness. Dyer was a clever young man and did eventually outwit his captors and return home where he married three times and left twenty-one children.

After nine days of marching, the group reached Logstown or a village on the Ohio River. Nicholas Seybert, James Dyer, and the other captives were distributed to various Indian villages. Young Adam Mallow was taken to Chillicothe and his sister, Mary, to another village. Their mother Anna Margaretha, however, was taken to a different village on the Ohio River near what is Portsmouth today. She was an excellent seamstress and was of value to the French to whom she was eventually sold, according to another story.

There are two accounts of Anna Mallow's release from the Indians. One states that she, with other prisoners, was forced to march to the Mississippi River. There she was sold to some French fur traders. Her son, Henry, was born November 18, 1758, on a fur trader's barge on the Mississippi. She was evidently pregnant when she was captured. She and Henry were held in French captivity in Louisiana before making their way home. Henry's application for pension for service in the Revolutionary War, lends support to this tradition. He states that he was born somewhere on the Mississippi River in 1758 while his mother was a captive of the French.

Another version suggests that Henry, the Mallow son, was born in the Indian village of Chillicothe. When he was born, the Indians doused him in a stream to wash off the taint of white blood to make a good Indian. Henry was the first white child born in Ohio according to this account. After a few years, the Indians wandered near New Orleans when the mother, daughter, and Henry were sold to the French and taken to Montreal.

The most logical explanation is as follows. On February 26, 1761, one Reverend Wilhelm reported that there was a Mrs. Mallow held captive in Montreal. This letter indicates that Mrs. Mallow and son were in Montreal by 1761 and probably released that year when Montreal fell to the English. By 1763 the French and Indian War had ended, and many captives were released. It is not certain when fourteen year old Mary returned home, but it was probably around 1763. One story states that Mary was returned to Fort Pitt by fur traders and then sent home. That the Mallows had returned home before 1765 is certain because Mallow's ad states so.

According to another source, arriving home just in time, Anna Margaretha was reunited with her husband who was just about to take another wife. No proof of this story exists, and, if she recorded her experiences, no record has been found. Reunited, the Mallows had at least two more children, Michael and Barbara, who are documented in Augusta County records.

After his wife, daughter, and Henry's return, Michael Mallow placed the following ad in the ***Pennsylvania Gazette*** on June 27, 1765, for the return of his son Adam. This document is a firsthand source and clearly states the number of Mallow children and the return of his wife and daughter. It also states that the family was taken at Fort Seybert, not at their cabin as some sources suggest.

Michael Mallow's ad

Seven years ago, the wife and 5 children of Michael Mallo, living on the south branch, in Augusta County, in Virginia, were taken prisoners by the Indians, when some time after, the three youngest children died, and the Wife and eldest Daughter came home again; but his Son, John Adam Mallo, was, according to the Report of other Prisoners, delivered up by the Indians but last Fall 1764.

Mallow did not mention the return of his young son Henry. Several family histories state that Mallow hated Indians the rest of his life, and some believe that he doubted his son Henry's parentage. However, DNA studies recently indicate that Henry was, indeed, a Mallow. Henry was included in his father's will.

Adam had remained in Ohio with the Shawnees in the village of Chillicothe. In the fall of 1764, Colonel Henry Bouquet made peace with the Indians and secured the release of three hundred Indian captives. These captives were brought to Ft. Pitt where many families were reunited with their lost children. Several of these captives did not want to be returned since they had grown to accept, even love, their Indian families. Adam Mallow was among these captives and refused to tell his name.

Those who were not claimed were eventually taken to Philadelphia where an exchange of prisoners was held in the fall of 1765. Adam, now fourteen years old, was one of these prisoners. By this time, Adam had forgotten or refused to say both his name and the English language. According to one story, one of Adam's father's neighbors was present in order to look for his missing daughter. This neighbor had been informed by Mallow, of certain scars on Adam's head and hand. The neighbor recognized Adam by these means.

Mallow immediately went to Philadelphia and reclaimed his son after seven years. He had, no doubt, thought his son was dead. It is said that Adam Mallow was brought back to his home in chains for fear he would run away to the Indians. Many captives did not want to return to their white families; however, Adam's history suggests he eventually became a part of his white family.

Some believe that Michael Mallow's hatred of the Indians remained the rest of his life. There was also the rumor that Adam Mallow was the only true son of Michael when Michael died intestate in 1772 suggesting that some settlers did not believe Michael Mallow to be the father of Henry. Today, it is proven that Henry was a Mallow, not an Indian as some have believed over the years, but rumors must have persisted among neighbors years after her return. Unfortunately, Anna did not record her experiences, and she may have been illiterate and still a predominantly German speaker.

Anna Margaretha Mallow did not survive very long after her return home. No doubt she suffered a great deal having lost three children and, perhaps, the affection of her husband when she returned with a son born in captivity. Having been reunited with her family for less than four years, she died before 1768 when Michael sold land, the deed lacking a spousal signature as required. She may have had three more children after her return and died in childbirth as was common. Sadly, her life must have been extremely difficult, even after her return. Michael married again; the name of a spouse called Mary appears on his estate sale.

Mallow had claimed 470 acres on Mallows Run in 1761 and died intestate before November 21, 1772, at age fifty two when his estate was entered into probate. A widow Mallow was listed as receiving items. The second wife was believed to be Mary Ingle as shown by a marriage record in 1769. Son Adam was administrator of his father's estate which could not be settled until the youngest child reached twenty one on November, 1779. This child was Henry.

Killbuck's last raid against the settlers may have been the taking of Fort Seybert. For some reason he became aligned with the Americans, perhaps due to the influence of the Christian Moravians. During the American Revolution Chief Killbuck and several members of his Delaware tribe, who supported the Americans, lived on a small island across from Wheeling. Two weeks after the savage murders of the Moravian Indian converts at Gnadenhutten in Ohio in 1781, Killbuck and his band feared retaliation from hostile tribes including the bulk of the remaining Delaware.

On March 24, Killbuck requested Colonel Brodhead of the American forces to take him and others to Ft. Pitt for safety. They were later attacked by those who wished retaliation, but Killbuck escaped the island in a canoe and was put by Col. Brodhead in the Wheeling guard house for safety.

That night, seventeen year old Lewis Wetzel and friend Boggs decided to kill Killbuck. They snuck into the guardhouse where Wetzel savagely tomahawked the chief. No charges were ever brought against Wetzel, and Killbuck was thrown into the Ohio River.

The settlers hated the Indians and refused to blame Wetzel for the killing. Wetzel's father had been killed by Indians earlier, and that instilled a lifelong hatred in the man who became a noted, but perhaps paranoid, Indian fighter, according to Alan Eckert, historian and author.

Killbuck's son, John Henry Killbuck Jr. was born in 1737 in Pennsylvania. Killbuck's daughter is believed to have married Leonard Schoolcraft, a white captive, who later helped the Indians raid and massacre the Hacker settlement in Virginia. John Killbuck Jr. was later converted to Christianity by the Moravians and supplied intelligence during the American Revolution. He argued for a neutral stand at that time, but some of the Delawares said no causing a tribal rift. In 1809 he signed the Ft. Wayne Treaty. He died in 1811 at age seventy four in Indiana where the Delawares had moved.

The grandson of Chief Killbuck became chief in 1811 after his father's death and was granted a pension and his son' rifles by the US government. They lived in Indiana where, in 1819, twenty three hundred Delaware Indians lived on the White River.

After returning home after the French and Indian War ended, Michael and Anna Margaretha's daughter Mary married Jacob Heavener in 1765. Jacob's mother, Elizabeth Seybert Heavener, had most likely been at Fort Seybert but escaped.

Adam Mallow, reunited with his family, continued to live in Virginia, none the worse for his over six years with the Shawnees. From 1766 until the start of Dunmore's War in 1774, the area now known as Pendleton County remained relatively peaceful. The reunited Mallows continued to farm their claim until Anna Margaretha died around 1768. She may have not reached her fortieth birthday and had given birth to at least eight children.

Adam's father had remarried by 1769. During that year the Reformed and Lutheran Congregations united and built a new church. George Mallow, Adam's uncle, was an elder, and Adam's father Michael was a member of the congregation

Although Michael Mallow died intestate in 1772, his estate was not settled until his youngest child was twenty one. His goods were sold on November 16, 1779, twenty one years after Henry, his youngest child was thought to have been born on the Mississippi River while his mother was a captive of the French.

Fred Keister and son Adam Mallow were administrators of the Mallow estate. Mallow's daughter Mary Heffenor (Hevener) bought two bags of spice, a large Bible, a pewter basin, and three plates. Her husband, Jacob Heffenor (Hevener) bought a black mare for 30 pounds and an officer's spear. Son Adam bought a hammer and anvil, cross cutsaw, ax, two bridles, a plough, a bay horse, a black mare, a great coat, trousers, half bushel of salt, a frying pan, and pewter spoons, among other items.

The widow Mallow, Mary Ingles, bought fourteen yards of linen, a tablecloth, towels, stockings, sheets, and a woman's saddle among other items. She then disappeared into history. There are records of Michael Mallow's affair with a neighbor and the birth of a child suggesting that Mallow was not content with his second wife or he never recovered from the loss of three of his children and his first wife. Today, we could not imagine the losses he incurred nor can we judge his feelings at such loss.

In 1774 Adam, former captive, married Sarah Bush, born in 1754, a daughter of another old Virginia family who had settled in the same area and discussed earlier. The couple continued to live on Mallow's run as did Henry, Adam's brother. Adam's education was very limited, and he may have been illiterate.

Indian problems resurfaced in 1773 and 1774The Governor of Virginia, Lord Dunmore, called out the colony's militia to crush the Indian tribes for once and for all. During 1774 the famous battle of Point Pleasant took place near what is now Pt. Pleasant on the Ohio River. Adam Mallow participated along with many of the local militia and also fought with the Virginia Militia in the Revolutionary War as did his brother Henry. Henry served in Colonel Benjamin Harrison's Regiment. According to a neighbor who passed down her information, Adam was very distressed having seen his Indian companions killed, perhaps by him. He maintained fond memories of his Indian home and often expressed the desire to return to Ohio when he could.

By the end of the Revolutionary War, Adam and wife Sarah had four children including Adam Junior born in 1778 and Henry, born in 1788, and continued to live on Mallow's Run. Brother Henry had also married, continued to live on his father's land, and had several children.

In 1806, Adam Senior, Adam Junior and brother Henry, named after his Uncle Henry, decided to move to Ohio, Ross County, the site where Adam Senior had spent over six years. Tradition suggests that Adam Sr. loved the Ohio country and was desirous of settling near his Indian home. He was fifty five years old and son Adam, born in 1778, was twenty eight when their families made the long, arduous journey to Ohio. Brother Henry, named after his uncle, was eighteen and came also.

The families settled on land in Ross County near a spring he remembered, and the Shawnee were long gone by then. The Mallows were industrious and successful farmers in Ross County and were among the earliest settlers. Adam Sr. died in 1841 at age ninety. Wife Sarah Bush died in 1850 at age ninety six, and both are buried in Fayette County, once part of

Ross. Their land is still farmed by their descendants.

Both Adam Jr. and Henry, and their sons, remained in Ohio, and left descendants. Henry married Sarah Popejoy, born in 1788, the daughter of John Popejoy and Mary Ann Champ, both born in Virginia. There are no records of this marriage which probably took place in Ohio, not Virginia, since the Popejoys were residents of Ohio when the Mallows came. Six children were born to Henry and Sara Popejoy. Mallow according to Fayette County histories. A 1830 census record shows Henry and Sarah had four daughters, but only three are noted in histories.

Adam Jr. and brother Henry fought in the War of 1812 and had many children. Henry died in 1848 and Sarah in 1871 at age eighty five and are buried along with other Mallows in Mallow Cemetery.

Henry's daughter Nancy, born in 1816, married William Bush in Ross County, Ironically, William Bush also descended from Adam Sr. wife's family. The couple were second cousins by descent from Lewis Bush from Germany, also an early settler. Nancy, William and son William died in Sedgwick

County, Kansas, where they had moved shortly after 1880. It is unknown why they moved to the frontier of Kansas but was probably due to land opportunities. Nancy died in 1891 and William in 1894 and are buried in the El Paso Cemetery.

Nancy and William's daughter Sarah married into another old Ross County family when she married Franklin Calvin Finch. The couple remained in Ohio.

George Mallow, son of George Mallow Sr. who was Michael Mallow's brother, was among the earliest settlers in Greene County, Ohio, where Germans from the South Fork area of Virginia settled. He was Adam Mallow Sr.'s cousin.

Lambert

The Lamberts, another German family, came to the Colony of Pennsylvania and moved west, spending a generation in the South Branch area of Virginia. Their paths crossed with the Bushes, Mallows and Riffles.

The name Lambert is often English in origin; however, the name is also derived from the Lombard tribe located in northern Germany as early as 500 AD. One early immigrant, Jacob Matthias Lombard, probably descended from this Lombard clan and was born in the Upper Rhine Valley in eastern France or Northern Germany. According to most sources, Matthias, as he was called, was born around 1690, perhaps in Baye Pfalz Bayan, in eastern France. In 1714 he married Anna Reesin or Rees also born in the same area. This family emigrated from Switzerland on the ship *Sally* in 1733 with sons: George, born in 1715, and John Jacob, born in 1716 according to a Pennsylvania court record. Their immigration may have been due to the persecution of the French Huguenots.

The Lamberts were Lutheran and emigrated with other German-French seeking freedom of religion and safety from persecution during the Reformation in Europe. The colony of Pennsylvania offered sanctuary and encouragement to these German settlers.

By 1734 Matthias owned one hundred acres of land in Manchester, Dover Township, York County, Pennsylvania, and was a farmer. Several more children were born in Pennsylvania including Jacob, Anna, Marie, John, Casper, and Catherine, the last born in 1735. Matthias was listed in several York County, Pennsylvania, records as guardian to several children including one Henry Habocher.

Also, in 1737 Matthias appeared in the court of Chester County attesting to the birth of his son John Jacob in 1716 in Germany. He managed to secure this son's release from William Moor to whom John Jacob was sold as an indentured servant until age twenty one. John Jacob must have been close to the end of his term of indenture; and his father, for a sum, secured his freedom. The indenturing of children was not uncommon because families often lacked enough money to pay for their passages from Europe. It would seem that Matthias Lambert had found it necessary to indenture his oldest son in order to pay for his passage.

On May 18, 1742, Matthias and wife Anna were sponsors at the baptism of Matthias Walther at Christ Lutheran Church, York Borough. Perhaps the child was named after his sponsor.

During this time men were required to work on roads, and in 1747 Matthias helped lay out a road to Philadelphia. He took the Oath of Allegiance on April 10, 1748, at Philadelphia along with other Lamberts. He also received a land warrant from Pennsylvania on May 14, 1750.

By 1755 the French and Indian War was well underway, and Lambert became a member of Christian Kauffman's Company, Dover Township militia. During that year settlers were killed and children carried away. Raiding parties of five to twenty Indians often appeared at night, scalped settlers and stole children. On Christmas Day of that year penniless refugees with clothes in rags congregated at the LeFevre Tavern in Manchester deciding their futures.

By 1756 only ninety-eight families remained in Dover Township, and over three hundred farms were empty. Three hundred people had been killed in Pennsylvania, according to Early **German Settlers of York County, PA** (Keith A. Dull). Matthias wrote his will on June 27, 1756, and it was probated March 16, 1757. Like many of his German neighbors, Lambert was killed by the Indians in late February or early March 1757. The circumstances of his murder are not clear, but he may have died while serving with the militia.

The family no doubt suffered as did hundreds of other pioneer families. Matthias was around sixty-seven years old when he was killed. His oldest son George had moved to Frederick County, Maryland, by 1744 when he bought land. Matthias's widow Anna moved to that area after the death of her husband. Her will was probated in 1758 indicating she did not live long after Matthias' death. She, too, was in her sixties. Son John Jacob remained in Dover Township, York County, Pennsylvania. Other children also remained in Pennsylvania including Anna, Marie, John and Casper whose children left many descendants.

Matthias' first-born son George S. came to America at age fifteen with parents and brother in 1733. At age twenty, George met and married Eva Catherine Jesserang, the daughter of Bartholomew and Anna Maria Jesserang. She was born April 15, 1722, in Germany and must have been only fourteen years old at the time of her marriage. She gave birth to her first child John in 1736 in Maryland where the couple resided. It is doubtful the couple had much education; they could not write. They were Lutheran as were most German immigrants in the area and spoke German.

From 1742 to 1755, George owned land in Frederick County, Maryland, that became known as "Lambert's Delight". George also owned twenty two acres called "Lambert Park" in 1744. The couple at that time had son John born in 1736 and daughter Eva Marie in 1739. Later, in 1746, son George was born. There may have been other children but their names are not recorded, and they may have died as did many infants at the time.

On March 21, 1778, George enlisted and fought in the Revolutionary War in Colonel Grayson's Regiment in Maryland. He was in his early sixties. Wife Eva Catherine died in 1781 in Washington County, Maryland, and is probably buried in Lambert Park. George died in 1787 at age seventy-two and is presumably buried in same place.

Although there is no definitive proof that John B. Lambert was the son of George Lambert, the fact that they lived next to one another suggests the relationship as do the naming patterns of the family. John is not mentioned in George's will; however, he had moved to Augusta County, now West Virginia, as early as 1770, according to some family genealogies. Perhaps John and his father had differences. George Jr. also left Maryland for Virginia. Since neither son was mentioned in George's will, one might speculate that the sons left Maryland under bad circumstances with their father. Then, too, they may have received their shares earlier allowing their moves.

John B., the oldest child of George and Eva Catherine, was born in 1736 near Hagerstown, Maryland, on his parents' farm. Around 1755 twenty-year old John married Joanna or Jeanette Heinrich and lived on land adjoining George Lambert's Lambert Park. As had many others, John and Joanna decided to move the sparsely settled area of the Virginia frontier in 1770. His parents remained in Maryland.

As early as the 1750s this area provided refuge for deserters from the French and Indian War as well as opportunities for land. John left the area where he was the son of a prosperous farmer and stood to inherit with one additional brother George who, ironically, also left the area to move to the frontier Tygart Valley of Virginia.

According to *The History of the Lambert Family*, John bought twenty five acres known as Gordon's Chance on November 12, 1762, this land lying in Cumberland County, Pennsylvania. On January 3, 1769, Lambert sold the Pennsylvania land for 100 pounds. He had paid 18 pounds for it. By that time he had settled in Wilson's Ridge on the Tygart River in Augusta County, Virginia.

It is presumed the family left Maryland and traveled to York, Pennsylvania. After a period of time they then took the Forbes Road to Western Pennsylvania, then south to the Tygart River Valley, a long trip. Lambert eventually sold eighteen acres in 1771 in Frederick County, and his wife Jean signed the deed.

There is no record Lambert bought land in the Tygart Valley. He soon moved from

Wilson's Station to what is now Pendleton County, West Virginia. It is likely that Lambert, as well as his son James, fought with the Augusta Militia at the famous battle of Point Pleasant in October of 1774. One record from the <u>History of Pendleton County, W VA</u> (1981 Morton, Owen p. 385) states John Lambert was exempt from military service by reason of physical infirmity, perhaps from an injury at this battle. He would have been in his late forties.

Records show Lambert had patented two hundred acres on Dry Run, Pendleton County, in 1783. The list of tithables in Pendleton County for 1790 lists John B. Sr., John Jr. and James. In 1804, John B. wrote his will and died on January 19, 1804, leaving several children including Matthias, James, born in 1757, Garnett, Abraham, Barnett, George, Jane, Suzanne and Catherine.

John's brother George and George's son, John Jr., were less than ideal husbands. Brother George took up with one Jane Warner for a decade and had several children known as Warners. Although he never married Jane Warner, these children later referred to themselves as Warners who were really

Lamberts. George then married Nelly Johnson and had other children.

John Junior left his first wife Nancy and their children to run off with Winnie Nelson Summerfield. Winnie was married to Joseph Summerfield, an early settler, who had been shipped to America from England for stealing along with his brother. In 1799 Summerfield was awaiting trial in Virginia for stealing ten dollars. Wife Winnie began "fooling around" with neighbor John Lambert, and husband Joseph was sentenced to two years in prison. In 1801 Winnie had Lambert's son Caleb, and in 1802 the couple took off to Tennessee where they had additional children through 1812.

John Sr.'s son, James B., was born in Maryland in 1758. It is unclear what the B. stood for. James with parents and siblings settled in what is the Tygart Valley in the 1770s. When he was sixteen, James, along with his father, fought at the Battle of Point Pleasant. He had enlisted for a period of three months. After the battle, the Lamberts moved from Wilson Station to the South Branch of the Potomac River, known as German Valley. At that time James Lambert enlisted for another three month period in the Virginia Militia from

July through October at age seventeen. In 1775-6 James fought a third time as a substitute for Jacob Ellsworth, a neighbor. This tour took him to the Battle of Great Bridge. He was discharged by Colonel William Crawford who would later be cruelly burned at the stake when captured by the Indians in Ohio. In 1779 both James and older brother Matthias enlisted and fought in the Revolutionary War for Virginia for a period of over two years. James was twenty-one by this time. He fought at the Battle of Cowpens as well as the Battle of Guilford Court House in 1781.

Records of James Lambert's marriages are unclear; however, one family record states that James married a Jane Wamsley in Maryland. Family tradition records her name as Wamsley, the daughter of William Wamsley, another Revolutionary War veteran of Virginia.

In 1804 James Lambert is listed as the stepfather of William Wamsley at the latter's marriage in Kentucky suggesting that Jane Wamsley must have been a widow with children. A record in Pendleton County mentions James and wife Margaret, not Jane, suggesting that James, too, may have been a widower when he married Margaret. A later census record indicates James had a son James Jr. who would have been older than William Wamsley. Although there is scant evidence, there is every reason to believe James was married in the early 1780s when he was in his twenties. There is also reason to believe that James and first wife had son James Jr. and a daughter Naomi for whom James also signed the marriage bond years later. There were also Wamsleys residing in Augusta County where James probably met the widow Wamsley.

Sometime after the Revolutionary War, James, and brothers Abraham and Matthias, set out for Kentucky, still a part of Virginia, as early as 1783. However, James and Margaret were recorded in a litigation suit in Augusta County in 1788 suggesting they did not move to Kentucky until after that. James Lambert is also on the list of tithables in 1790 although he could have left for Kentucky shortly before that.

The area of Kentucky where the Lambert brothers settled as early as 1788 was a very dangerous place. John Bradford, founder of the first Kentucky newspaper, The Kentucky Gazette, in 1787, compiled extensive notes on both the social and political issues confronting the not yet a state, Kentucky. Bradford writes "In the year 1788, the northern and southern frontiers of Kentucky were infested by the Indians; its inoffensive citizens were bleeding under the tomahawk and the scalping knife…[and] could obtain no protection from their government. . ." (113).

Among many, Bradford describes a massacre in March 1788 where three boats descending the Ohio River were attacked by the relentless Shawnee. A few men escaped from one flat boat but no one from the other two was ever seen again and presumed killed. In May another boat was found drifting near Louisville covered with blood and all aboard were killed. In November, attacks occurred on the road from Limestone to Lexington and near Blue Licks.

Problems continued in 1789. In May two boys were killed near Limestone and a woman and child killed on the Beargrass River; horses were stolen. In June, two men were killed on the Elkhorn River, two men near Crab Orchard, and a hunter killed near Bullitt's Lick. At the end of November, Isaac Sollars was killed and scalped while hunting on the Licking River.

In 1790, General Harmer mounted an offensive against the Miami Indians who lived where Ft. Wayne is now. Twelve hundred Kentucky militia participated and were eventually confronted by 700 Indians. The detachment immediately gave way and fled, pursued by the enraged Indians. In the end, the bedraggled army returned to Ft. Washington. It was reported the Kentucky militia was ineffective at best. The Indians continued harassing and killing Kentucky settlers.

Although Kentucky became a state in 1792, the Indian threat continued for several more years. In 1793, Bradford reported that "John Haggard was killed and scalped six miles from Nashville. Twelve balls were shot into him. His wife was killed last summer by the Indians and he has left five small children in poverty and wretchedness" (191). The Indians continued to steal horses. Eighteen were stolen from Jefferson County, and cattle and hogs were killed. A boat destined for Illinois was taken near the mouth of the Ohio and sixteen men were killed, "their heads and hands cut of, and bodies ripped open" (195).

Finally, on August 3, 1795, The Treaty of Greenville was concluded and things began to improve for the Kentucky settlers, some of whom were anxious to cross the Ohio River and settle the fertile lands of Ohio. The Lambert men may likely have joined local militia at various times in pursuit of the Indians during their first few years in Kentucky. They may have crossed paths with Daniel Boone at Boonesborough or Simon Kenton during this time. In any event, they were no strangers to danger and fear from Indian raids. Their wives, too, were subjected to fear and depredation during these bloody years.

From the standpoint of the twenty first century, it is extremely difficult to understand the motives and daring of these early Kentucky settlers. No doubt they envisioned future prosperity and land ownership. Many, like James Lambert, continued moving west to Indiana. And before he died there, James had purchased over 30,000 acres in Illinois in the 1840s but never made that final move. He died in 1847 having lived a long life during very dangerous times. What happened to the Illinois land is not clear.

There is no doubt that at least four sons of John B. Lambert lived in Kentucky by 1790 and were following in their father's wanderlust. The first record of James in Kentucky occurs in 1789 on Jefferson County tax list. The 1790 Kentucky census shows that James lived in Jefferson County, Matthias in Clark County, Abraham in Nelson County and Barnett, another brother, in Bourbon County. From 1803 to 1807 James and wife owned twenty five and a half acres on Paint Lick Creek in Madison County, Kentucky. Also, in 1804 in Madison County, one Naomi Lambert married Eden Bayles with James signing the marriage bond. It is probable that this was James' daughter by the first wife. Brother Matthias married Elizabeth Williams in 1796 and also received a Revolutionary War pension in 1834. Matthias and wife also sold land bordering on George Lambert's land In Madison County. They signed with x's indicating they could not write.

For at least thirty years James B. and second wife, Margaret, lived in Kentucky. The 1810 census lists one James, over forty five years of age, a wife over forty five, one son under ten (Noah), one son ten to fifteen, one son sixteen to twenty-five, and one daughter between ten and fifteen. This census record suggests that James had five children. The family lived in Madison County, Kentucky, where Mathew (Matthias), James' brother resided. Records also show George and William Lambert in the same county, and there is reason to believe that the men were related.

By 1807 Matthias had died in Madison County and is listed as the son of John B. Lambert. James and Margaret's youngest child, Noah, was born in 1805 in Madison County when James was around forty-seven years old. By 1820, only Noah remained at home with his widowed father.

Margaret died before 1820 when James appears in Dearborn County, Indiana, in the 1820 census with just one son Noah. Census records show Noah's mother was alive in the 1810 but not in 1820 when James and Noah lived in Indiana. The 1820 Indiana census also lists a James Junior and a Nathanial. These men might very well have been siblings of Noah. The 1820 Kentucky census lists George, Matthias, Abraham, Garrett, and William still residing in Kentucky and the birth dates of these men in later census records substantiates their family connection.

Also in the Dearborn, Indiana, census was listed Jane Kaiser Neely, a widow with three children. James made her acquaintance and married her in 1822 in Ohio or Indiana. She was thirty-seven and he was sixty-five. Two daughters, Lucinda in 1824 and Phoebe in 1827, were born of this union. The family was in Columbia Township, Hamilton County, Ohio, by 1830 but moved back to Indiana around 1837 when James purchased land in Indiana. James also purchased six parcels of land in Illinois from 1840-1846. The family did not move to Illinois, however. The fate of the 32,000 acres James purchased is unknown, and James lived until 1847 at age ninety-one in Dearborn County, Indiana. The widow Jane then followed some of her children to Iowa where she died and is buried.

Noah Lambert married his stepsister, Elizabeth Neely, in 1826 in Dearborn County, Indiana, or Hamilton County, Ohio.

The third wife of James B. Lambert, Jane Kaiser, was born in 1785. One record suggests she was Christina Jane Kaiser of Germany. On February 1, 1805, Jane had married John Neely, son of Peter Neeley, in Ovid, New York. Peter Neely was an Irishman who was born in 1761.

His son John was born in 1783 at Fort Schlosser, Canada. Jane was only nineteen or twenty at the time of her marriage to Neely. Within eight months, October 4, 1805, Jane gave birth to son Louis, who later followed the Mormons to Vermillion and Nauvoo, Illinois, and died in Salt lake City, a Mormon.

Jane and John Neely's daughter Elizabeth was born in 1807, Nancy in 1809, and Mary, born in 1811, who married a Woods in 1830 in Dearborn County. All four of Jane Neeley's children were born in New York. In 1812 John Neeley was killed at Ft. Seneca, during the War of 1812 leaving wife Jane with four children under seven years of age. He was a volunteer with the New York Rifleman Company as a Private.

The widow, Jane Neeley, came to Randolph Township, Dearborn County, Indiana by 1820. For a widow with such young children to move from New York to the newly settled Indiana suggests she came with family rather than alone. By 1822 Jane, age thirty seven, met and married the much older James B. Lambert. James had seventeen year old son Noah, and Jane had a fifteen year old daughter, Elizabeth.

Within three years Noah Lambert and Elizabeth Neely married, probably in Hamilton County, Ohio, where they resided in 1830. Jane and James had two children, Lucinda, born in 1824 and Phoebe in 1827, both born in Hamilton County, Ohio. The family had moved to the Colerain area after their marriage. By 1840 they were back in Indiana. In 1846 James died in Dearborn County, leaving Jane a widow again.

Noah, son of James and Jane Lambert was born in 1805 in Kentucky. Noah was about fifteen or younger at the time of his father's move to Indiana. His older siblings either stayed in Kentucky or moved independently to Indiana. James Junior is listed in the census separately from Noah and his father and was probably an older half-brother. In 1822 Noah, age seventeen and James, either his father or brother, were mentioned in a law suit. By 1825 or so, Noah had married his stepsister Elizabeth Neely and lived in Columbia, Hamilton County, Ohio.

Noah and Elizabeth had the following children. William, 1826, John N 1829, Richard 1834, Valentine 1838, Samuel 1844, and Eliza 1849. One daughter, Margaret burned to death as a little girl. In 1840 the family was still in Hamilton County in Colerain Township. By 1850, they had moved back to Ohio County, Indiana. Noah died around 1852 in southern Indiana when he was thrown from a horse and killed at age forty seven. Elizabeth lived until 1868 when she died in Muscatine County, Iowa, where she had moved after Noah's death. Several of her younger children as well as her mother Jane moved to Iowa also.

The son of Noah and his stepsister, Elizabeth Neely, John Neely Lambert, was born on December 26, 1829, in Hamilton County, Ohio. In 1854, the family settled in Delaware County, and later owned a farm near Daleville, Salem Township. Lambert's obituary sates that "soon after marriage, the family moved near Daleville, Indiana, and lived there the whole time." John Neely Lambert married Nancy Jane Graham on March 17, 1853, when she was twenty-four. The couple had nine children including Mary Elizabeth, Joseph Orange, James Allen, John, William, David Arthur, Charles Edgar, Olive Perry, Oscar Clay, and Josie Bell. Nancy lived until June 1, 1907. John Neely died June 1, 1907, the cause of death being senility according to his death certificate. He was seventy-eight years old. Nancy had died February 18, 1879, thirty years before her husband, and both are buried near Daleville, Indiana.

John Neely's obituary reads as follows:

John N. Lambert was born December 26, 1829, and departed this life June 1, 1907, aged 77 years, 5 months, and 5 days. He was united in marriage with Nancy J. Graham, March 27, 1853, To this union were born nine children, seven sons and two daughters, all of whom except one son, James A. who died March 16, 1885, survive him. The surviving children are Mary E. Hoffman, of Gaston, Indiana, Joseph O., Washington D. C., John W. Gaston, Indiana, David A., Muncie, Indiana; Oliver Pr., Lexington, Oklahoma; Charles E., Muncie, Indiana; he is survived also by one brother, Samuel Lambert, of Cedar Edge, Colorado, one sister, Eliza Jewell of Peru, Nebraska, all of whom, except one so, Oliver P. of Oklahoma, were present at the funeral. The deceased was born of Noah and Elizabeth Lambert, in Hamilton County, Ohio, where he was married. Soon after their marriage more than fifty years ago, they moved to Delaware County, setting, then an almost unbroken forest in the vicinity south of Daleville, where he lived continuously up to the time of his death. With his devoted wife he lived happily, toiling early and late, as the pioneers were want to do, making a home for the family which came to his home, an providing the children the means and opportunity for an education to the extent of his ability.

Riffle

The Riffles were among the Germans who sought better lives in America in the middle 1700s. This family has a most colorful history. Some were also infamous in their pursuits, and others were very successful. Their wives were their matches, and one is immortalized in stone in Randolph County, West Virginia. The early generations of Riffles pursued their interests and were extremely pragmatic.

By 1746, a Jacob Riffle lived in Berks County, Pennsylvania, and obtained a land grant. Matthias Riffle also lived in Berks at the time, both adults with wives and children. Their relationship to the following Jacob Riffel is not clear, but the names suggest they were kin.

In 1750 the ship *Phoenix* arrived in Philadelphia. Among its passengers were Jacob Riffel, born in 1725, and at least two sons, including Jacob Jr., born in 1745, and his brother Matthias. Jacob's wife's name was thought to be Catherine, but a later Pennsylvania record records her name as Martha. The Riffel families settled in the

German area of Pennsylvania and remained there for over a decade.

By 1765 the Riffels (Riffles) lived in German Township, Fayette County. By 1768, Jacob built Riffle's Fort that later became Riffle's Lutheran Church. Jacob Jr. was five when he came to American with his parents and grew up with several brothers.

By 1772, Jacob Jr., now twenty-seven years old, took his family to the Virginia frontier. His father Jacob remained in Pennsylvania where he died around 1790 and was buried in Jacob's Lutheran Church Cemetery. Several of his children and his nephews and nieces continued to live in Pennsylvania as did numerous descendants of the earlier immigrant Jacob, causing much confusion in the tracing of Riffle ancestry.

According to a letter belonging to the estate of Harold Jones, Jones' great, great grandfather Jacob Riffle (the son of the immigrant Jacob) came from Germany before the Revolutionary War at the age of five. There were three children who came also. Reportedly, Matthias went to Pennsylvania, one to Virginia (Jacob), and one to Ohio (George?). These were the sons of the immigrant Jacob.

Three Riffle men were recorded before the Revolutionary War. There were two Riffles at Ft. Pitt with the Virginia Militia, Matthias and George, during the French and Indian War. There was also a Jacob who was part of the Monongalia Militia E, all paid off for military service at Ft. Pitt in 1772. The latter was the Jacob Jr. discussed in this narrative. The relationship of these Riffles is unclear, partly because every Riffle family had a Jacob and a Matthais.

By 1772 Jacob Jr., son of the immigrant Jacob, had settled in the Tygart Valley on the Virginia frontier. He had married Dorothy Strunk and died in Lewis County in 1816. Dorothy, also born in 1745, died a year later in Braxton County. She was described in a letter found in the estate of Harold Jones: "great, great grandmother Dorothy is reported as being able to stand in a half bushel measure and shoulder a three bushel sack of wheat'" suggesting a large, strong woman well suited for a life with immigrant Jacob.

Jacob Riffle Jr. was among the first settlers in Randolph County, now West Virginia, and had settled by 1772 on a stream in the Huttonsville District. *The History of Clay*

County, West Virginia states that "Jacob and his brother Francis "Frank" Riffle were immigrants from Germany and moved their families across the mountains from "old" Virginia to the wilderness that was Tygart's Valley where they became first settlers of Randolph County".

The History of Randolph County, West Virginia (1875) states "Jacob Riffle. . . deserted from the Virginia Army during the French and Indian War. . . His son's name was Jacob and he, probably accompanied by his father, settled in the Tygart Valley" {171-2).

The History of Randolph County states that Jacob was deserter from service under George Washington during the French and Indian War and hid out in the Tygart Valley until the War ended in 1763; he settled on Riffle's Creek, a tributary of the Tygart River.

It is not clear why Jacob deserted or even if it is true. Accordingly, the Riffles made a camp in a hollow sycamore tree on Buckhannon River with another family of deserters, the Pringles, described earlier. There is no doubt that Riffles settled the area very early; however, whether they actually lived in the sycamore tree is open to question. Some believe that the deserter was Jacob Sr., the immigrant. If Jacob Sr. had deserted George Washington's forces before 1772, he eventually returned to German Township, Pennsylvania, where he died in 1790 and is buried in Jacob's Lutheran Church Cemetery.

The immigrant Jacob's son, Jacob Jr., fought with the Virginia Militia during the American Revolution. His pension record is recorded as VA 59066 in the National Archives. He was in Captain John Whitzell's Company in the Virginia Militia. Some believe that Jacob fought at Pt. Pleasant in 1774 and was with Col. William Crawford's forces who were massacred by Indians in Ohio later. The records of those who fought with Crawford are incomplete, but it is possible.

It is also recorded that the Riffles were among the first settlers in Randolph County and owned three hundred acres on Riffle Creek, named after the family. Later, Jacob and Dorothy moved to Braxton County, Virginia. In 1800 the family settled on O'Brien's Fork on the Saltlick River. The Riffles, Jacob Jr. and family, appear up in many histories and court records in Randolph County after 1772, and the family was still residing there in 1787 when Jacob's brother Francis was murdered by the Indians.

SIMS Index to Land Grants in West Virginia shows that Jacob Riffle Jr. was granted fifty acres along the Tygart River in 1791; three hundred acres in Randolph County in 1792; and one hundred and twenty four acres on Riffle's Run, also in Randolph. There are many deeds recorded showing Jacob's transfer of land to his children from 1791 – 1816. Francis, his brother, was killed between Becca's Creek and Riffle's Creek in Randolph County, a day after the Kinnan massacre in the same area. Before his death, Francis signed the petition to form a county government from Harrison County and to move the county seat closer to his home. Both Francis and his brother Jacob were actively involved in community affairs.

Once established in Virginia, Jacob and Dorothy Riffle had eleven children: Catherine, 1765; Dorothy, 1766; David, 1770; Jacob Jr., 1774; Christina, 1778; Francis, 1781; George, 1782; Elizabeth, 1780; Isaac, 1783; Peter: and Mary, many of whom left descendants. In 1817 Dorothy Riffle, the mother, was probably buried near Bulltown, West Virginia, where she lived with her son Francis (named for Uncle Francis killed by Indians) for the year she was a widow. Dorothy lived to approximately seventy-two years of age while Jacob, her husband, died a year earlier at age seventy-one, very respectable ages for the time.

Much later in 1835, Jacob's will was contested but also appeared listed in the Spring Term 1839. There was a land dispute lasting for many years. This will is remarkable in many respects as it describes the condition of his heirs. His children were listed as follows:

Mary Shaver, wife of George Shaver living somewhere in Ohio; Catherine Wilson, wife of George Wilson; David Riffle, Dead with children living in Ohio; Peter Riffle Dead left 2 children residence unknown; Christina Riffle Dead left 3 children viz. John N Riffle (a bastard); David O'Neil; Sarah Howell wife of Jonathan; Jacob Riffle; Francis Riffle; George Riffle, dead, his children and lawful wife living in Ohio. (He left his first wife and married a second by whom he had children who lived in Lewis Co.); *Isaac Riffle; Elizabeth Mace married Nicholas Mace alias Nicholas Wilmouth; Dorothy. . .*

Jacob and Dorothy had been dead for many years when the estate was finally settled, and most of their children had died by then also.

David, the oldest son and an early Ohio settler, became a prominent frontiersman and citizen; however, George Strunk Riffle, David's younger brother by ten plus years, was another story. He died at age thirty-one after service in the War of 1812. George married Margaret Helmick around 1803 in Virginia, and the couple with a young daughter Mary, moved to Montgomery County, Ohio, where George's brother David and family had settled. George did not fare well in Dayton and was forced to pay money for "goods stolen" at the store where he worked. George and Margaret were indigent which prompted Dayton trustees to take their young daughter Mary to be raised by Paul Butler, one of the trustees. Neither parent attempted to get the child back, and her fate is not known. The Butlers moved to northern Ohio after the War of 1812. These records can be viewed in Montgomery County, Ohio, chancery records.

Sometime in 1808, Margaret told her neighbors that George had left to hunt and never returned. She believed he had been killed by the Indians. It had been years since anyone had been killed by the Indians; however, some believed her tale. Lacking both a husband and funds, Margaret, who was pregnant, incurred much sympathy from her neighbors who aided her. She had another daughter, Deborah, who was raised by neighbors.

In the meantime, George had returned to Virginia where he married Susannah McColley, a woman of dubious reputation, thought to have had at least one illegitimate child before she married George. Jacob Sr., George's father, was furious and left Susannah and her three children nothing in his will.

Eventually, George appeared in the Virginia Militia at Ft. Pitt during the War of 1812 and was sent to Norfolk, Virginia, where he was severely wounded and died. His widow Susannah applied for his pension even though she was not his legal wife. In the meantime, Margaret had given birth to Deborah in Dayton, Ohio, but soon left the child with neighbors. There is no evidence she cared for either of her daughters by George Riffle. She eventually married James Murray Street, moved to Indiana and had several more children.

Deborah later married a much older man and moved to Utah where she is buried.

Then there was Peter Riffle, another brother, who was incarcerated in Harrison County, Virginia, where he died in jail. There is a record for payment to a guard for taking care of Peter before his death. Peter left two children who lived for a time with their grandparents, Jacob and Dorothy. One of these children was Barbara, who later married her first cousin, Jonathon Riffle, the son of George Strunk Riffle by Susannah McCalley. When Jacob's will was written, the whereabouts of these two children were not known. Evidently, Peter's wife was in no condition to care for her children when Peter died, and there is no record of her.

Jacob's will also mentions a bastard, John N. Riffle, with three children. Sons Jacob and Francis spent ten years fighting over the terms of their father's will which caused the long delay in its settlement. One of the brothers had sold his father's land and then denied it, saying it was only a loan. His brother did not view it that way, causing a long court dispute.

David, the oldest son, evidently was unaffected by the confusion because he had settled in Montgomery County, Ohio, by 1798, and never saw any of his brothers again, except for the unlucky George who came to Ohio for a few years before disappearing.

Jacob and Dorothy Riffle's first son David married a resourceful woman named Margaret Swisic Ward. She is one of the remarkable women of history and is mentioned numerous times in the history of West Virginia. She has been memorialized in a statue in Hoover Cemetery, Randolph County, for her courage.

Orphaned Margaret was raised in Hampshire County, Virginia, by the Thixton or Hixton family of that area. No other information has been found regarding her background. She was born February 15, 1767, in Virginia and married a Revolutionary War veteran called George Ward when she was fifteen on February 24, 1783. Margaret was eight years younger than George, a son of David and Susanna Ward, descendants of Captain John Ward of Jamestown fame.

The couple had three children: Mary, David, and George Jr. The unfortunate George Ward Sr. died suddenly in February of 1791 in Randolph County. He was only thirty-two years old and may have died of small pox. He was the nephew of the famous Sylvester Ward who fought at Yorktown and settled near Huttonsville in the Tygart Valley on the frontier.

Although the Revolutionary War had ended in 1783, raiding parties of Indians continued to plague Virginia, Pennsylvania, and Kentucky. The 1780s had been a very bloody time for America's frontier, and many settlers were killed by these raiding parties, consisting mostly of Mingoes and Shawnees. The western frontier of Virginia did not escape these raids. During dangerous times, families often "forted" together in order to protect themselves from Indian attacks.

On May 18, 1791, Margaret Ward, a widow for a scant three months, took her children to the cabin of Joseph Kinnan and his family for safety from possible Indian attacks. Kinnan was a neighbor.

There are several accounts of the story and, in addition, Mary Lewis Kinnan told her story to a printer in Elizabeth, New Jersey, who then published it as_ ***The True Narrative of the Sufferings of Mary Kinnan***.

Joseph and Mary Lewis Kinnan had opened their home to Margaret Ward and her children as well as Mary's brother. At the time of the fateful attack, there were at least a dozen people staying in the Kinnan cabin for safety.

Late one warm, pleasant day in May, the Kinnan cabin was attacked by a three Shawnees. There was no escape, and Joseph Kinnan was killed immediately. Mary Kinnan, watched in horror as one of her children was tomahawked, Desperate, she grabbed one of her younger children and a gun and fled outside. She then threw her baby over a crude fence into the bushes and prayed that it would remain silent. The child was too young to obey and followed its mother. The Indians pursued her while the remaining men in the cabin ran away leaving the women to their fate. Mary and her child were cornered by one of the Shawnees. Mary struck him over the head with the gun. The other Indians admired her courage and decided to take her captive rather than kill her. The child was killed at some point along the Indians' hasty journey to the safety of Ohio and Michigan.

While Mary was trying to protect herself and her child, Margaret Ward was able to escape to a back room of the small cabin with her two boys. Her daughter, Mary, had been savagely tomahawked to death at the initial attack, and her son George received a head wound. Running to a small ventilation opening, Margaret was able to push her sons through the opening and crawl through herself. Finding two terrified Kinnan children outside, she managed to secure all four children and run three miles to the safety of the nearest neighbor, John Hamilton. Ironically, the Kinnan massacre was the last Indian killing in what is now Randolph County, West Virginia. Margaret much later testified about the incident in Darke County, Ohio, when she applied for the Revolutionary pension on George Ward's service.

Meanwhile, Mary Kinnan's brother, Jacob, who was one of the men who had run away, leaving the women to defend themselves, returned to the cabin alone later that evening to discover the death and destruction from which he had fled. He must have been disgusted at his behavior because he relentlessly continued to try to locate his captive sister. In the meantime he returned to the Lewis family in New Jersey.

In 1795, four years later, a letter came to the Lewis family to which the brother of Mary Lewis Kinnan, the captive, had returned. The letter stated that Mary Kinnan was alive and living with a tribe of Delawares in Michigan, near Detroit. The letter had been written by a trader who had died of yellow fever and was buried with his belongings for fear of contagion. When his belongings were unearthed after a year, a letter was found concerning Mary's location. The trader had spoken with her while visiting the Delawares and heard her story.

For a year, Jacob planned and then executed his sister's release. Mary Lewis Kinnan was returned to her relatives and lived to be an old woman; however, after years of having to relate her awful experiences, she began to lose her mind and became delusional and paranoid. Sadly, she became known as "crazy old Aunt Polly".

The Riffles, Jacob and his brother Francis, lived in the same area. One day after the Kinnan massacre, Frank Riffle and others were traveling on road, believing that the Indians had left the area. They were wrong; Riffle and another man were killed, and several females of the family managed to escape on horseback.

The Riffles, Kinnans, and Wards were neighbors, so David Riffle knew the widow Margaret Ward. He married the widow in 1793 and took her and her two sons to Mason County, Kentucky, by 1794 where they remained until they could safely settle in the Ohio lands.

In July of 1939, a Riffle descendant found a letter in the Riffle family <u>Bible</u>; the letter indicated that Margaret and David went back to Hampshire County in 1793 to be married by the same Dunkard preacher who had married Margaret and George Ward ten years earlier. The census records of Mason County, Kentucky, show that David Riffle lived there during 1793-4. David and Solomon Riffle, whose relationship is not known, remained in Kentucky and settled Ohio when the opportunity presented. David and Margaret did not move to Montgomery County, Ohio, until 1796 or 7 and had two children by then. Their first child, Jacob, was born in the first year of their marriage. Margaret was a good match for her frontiersman husband and the life they would lead.

In any event, David Riffle, born in Virginia, moved to Kentucky, and then moved on to Montgomery County, Ohio, in 1796, with a wife and two young sons. Beer's *History of Montgomery County,* 1880, states ". . . *the father (David) came to Montgomery County in 1796 on a packhorse with two children . . . they were the second white family in the township. . ."*

The Riffles did not move to Ohio until they had purchased land in the Symmes Purchase. They were caught up in the Symmes land scandal and were forced to move from their original claim to another claim nearby. Descendants of David and Margaret Riffle are eligible for membership in the Old Northwest Territory Lineage Society because the author has proven their settlement before Ohio statehood.

According to Beers, *History of Darke County,* Richland Township, "The first settler was Jacob Hartell, followed nine months later, by David Riffle and his two sons Jacob and Soloman. The Riffles had remained near

Dayton, Ohio, until at least 1814 and did not move to the new Darke County until then.

Beers' History also states that David and Silas (David's nephew) Riffle were early settlers in Brown Township, Darke County. There is no mention of George and David Ward, Margaret's children from her first marriage, however, they were adults at the time and settled on their own. David and the two Riffle sons came shortly afterwards. The Ward brothers are mentioned in Darke County records and left descendants.

After the defeat of General St. Clair in November of 1791 at what later became Ft. Recovery, Ohio, as many as 1200 men were killed by a confederation of Indians. The Kentucky Militia was the first line of defense and failed miserably in holding the lines. The consequences were disastrous. David Riffle was probably still in Virginia at this time. In 1794, however, General Anthony Wayne was appointed by President Washington to succeed St. Clair.

Wayne sent out a call for men including Kentuckians. David Riffle, age twenty-four, answered the call since he was a resident of Mason County, Kentucky, at that time. These

Kentucky frontiersmen were well armed and well mounted; they no doubt were considered assets to Wayne's trained militia. In addition, they hated Indians because Kentucky had seen more than its share of Indian raids and massacres. Atrocities occurred on both sides, and the Kentuckians practiced scalping just as their enemies did. These frontiersmen did not enjoy good reputations.

Allen Eckert in *The Frontiersman*, an historical novel about Simon Kenton, a resident of Mason County, Kentucky, states that "..easterners assumed that only the dregs of society lived on the frontier." (183). Simon Kenton had resided near Limestone, now Washington, Kentucky, since the 1790s. Kenton too served under Anthony Wayne in the Indian Wars and the War of 1812. It is probable that David Riffle knew and rode with Kenton during this time. It is also probable that David Riffle knew not only Kenton but also George Rogers Clarke, Daniel Boone, and Anthony Wayne.

Ft. Recovery, built on the site of St. Clair's defeat, provided the scene for a second battle on June 30, 1794. David Riffle participated as part of the Kentucky Militia.

Over 2000 warriors under Little Turtle of the Miamis and Blue Jacket of the Shawnees made a frontal attack on the fort. A two day battle ensued, and the Indians finally gave up their assault. Wayne went on the offensive but did not pursue the Indians once the battle ended. Evidently David Riffle was not wounded and returned to Kentucky.

When David Riffle moved to Kentucky and, later, Ohio, the area was very sparsely settled and untamed. For the most part, the first settlers of both northern Kentucky and southern Ohio came from Virginia, Pennsylvania, Maryland, New Jersey and the Carolinas. These settlers were not rich but rather desired to create new homes and modest wealth in a new land. They expected both danger and hardships; they expected hard labor. Early accounts of these pioneers include words such as brave, vigorous, industrious, hearty, active, loyal, generous, and hospitable.

The pioneers made use of the land and its provisions. The primary apparel for men was deer skin which was made into hunting shirts, pants, coats, leggings and moccasins. Women, too, wore this article. Shoes and boots were made of deer skin. Occasionally men might own a calico shirt and a woman a calico dress. Sometimes deer's hair was used in place of socks. Obviously, deer were plentiful.

Most pioneers married early and were hunters at an early age. Their food consisted of bear meat, venison and turkey. Their cabins were usually one room with an earthen floor and education was practically nonexistent. Many pioneers did not read nor write. In addition, the first settlers often were attacked by skin disease and sore eyes attributed to water. The spring brought influenza, and bloody flux occurred from green vegetables and unripe fruit. Although illness did occur, one pioneer stated that "we had not then the sickly hysterical wives, with poor, puny, sickly dying children" (Evans, Nelson W. and Stivers, Emerson, 1900 West Union, Oh).

In the 1700s, the State of Ohio was a vast wilderness, almost entirely covered with a forest of huge trees. There were no roads but rather paths made by the herds of buffalo that inhabited the wilderness. The human inhabitants, the Indians, used the creeks and rivers as their roadways. An occasional white man lived for a time with the Indians. French and English traders passed through the area;

white captives spent time in the Indian villages known then as Chillicothe and Piqua.

When David Riffle arrived in Ohio, he, Margaret and their children encountered the very early rigors of settlement in the Ohio Territory only recently somewhat safe from Indian attacks. In addition, sixteen years later Riffle fought during the War of 1812. The governor of Ohio called for volunteers to meet at Dayton, Ohio, and march to Detroit to investigate the murder of three men. David and others were captured by Major General Brock of the British Army. They were paroled and returned to Montgomery County. On August 22, 1812, another call was issued for 1200 men. David became part of Captain Steele's Dayton Militia and ordered to St. Mary's where he remained for the duration of the War and the defeat of Tecumseh in 1813 at the Battle of Fallen Timbers.

The History of Darke County,(Beers, 1880) states that David Riffle after the war, purchased land on the Stillwater, above where Beamsville now is, and removed there in 1814, and after the lapse of a few years, died there in 1820 (219). David was buried on his farm and was sixty years old at the time of his death. It was reported that he had not lost but one tooth and that occurred when he tried to pull a wooden ramrod from a gun with his teeth (Robert John Riffle's genealogy. Ancestry. Com). Riffle died suddenly, perhaps of Milk Fever, a devastating ailment during the time, caused by the foraging of animals in the forest. Ironically, the Indians recognized the plant that caused the contamination of milk, but they were long gone by the time many contracted the devasting fever.

David Riffle, whose father Jacob had fought in the American Revolution, was a very enterprising, adventurous frontiersman. He fought in the Indian Wars and the War of 1812. He did not live to see a son and several grandsons fight for the Union during the Civil War, one of whom, Aaron, died after the South's defeat at Appomattox Court House in June of 1865. Also a Civil War veteran, Aaron's brother, Chauncey's obituary reported that his grandfather David was with General Anthony Wayne at the Battle of Ft. Recovery in 1794. No proof exists of this fact, however, but records are inconclusive.

Margaret, David's widow, married Reverend John Wintermute in 1826 in Darke

County; she was fifty-nine. He died in 1844 leaving Margaret a widow for the third time; she was seventy-seven. Refusing his children's request that Wintermute be buried by his first wife Abigail, Margaret had him buried where she wished. She died November 6, 1845, in Darke County at age eighty-seven, and Wintermute's children then had their father reinterred next to Abigail. Evidently Margaret needed funds because she applied for a Revolutionary War pension through George Ward. It is these pension papers that clearly document her life and the life of David Riffle. She was granted her pension but did not live long enough to collect much of it.

Margaret's will dated September 6, 1845, named her five children, two Wards and three Riffles including son Jacob. She signed with her mark and could not write. Probably David Riffle, her first husband, could not write either. Neither had time for much education.

David Riffle experienced a great deal in his sixty years. His life was intertwined with the American Indians with whom he interacted, both in battle and during his early settlement in Ohio. He and his courageous wife Margaret persevered under tragic and dangerous circumstances. The rigors of military service and pioneer life no doubt hurried David's death. However, Margaret died a very old woman for her time and outlived three husbands.

Born less than a year after their marriage, Margaret and David's first son Jacob, named after David's father and grandfather, was born in Kentucky in 1793 and was only four when the family settled in Ohio. He came to Ohio with parents David and Margaret around 1797 and in 1818 located in Richland Township, Darke County, as the second white family of that township.

Jacob, too, participated in the War of 1812 along with his father and died in the fall of 1853; he was a farmer and married Mary Van Scoyk, a daughter of Aaron Van Scoyk, who settled in Darke County in the early 1800s. Jacob and Mary had nine children, and all are buried in the Ansonia and New Teegarden Cemeteries except for one, Aaron Riffle, who rests in Arlington National Cemetery. Jacob and Mary are also buried in the Ansonia Cemetery.

The Van Scoyks should be mentioned since their ancestor Arien Van Shaik settled

America by 1634 and resided on Long Island where he farmed and supplied New Amsterdam with produce. His descendant, Aaron Van Scoyk, moved his family to Ohio from Kentucky in the early 1800s. Unlike the Riffles, this family waited to settle Ohio until it was safer. They resided in Montgomery and Greene County before moving to Darke County where Aaron purchased farm land. His sons, Joseph, William and John were in Ohio and enlisted in the War of 1812. The family farmed and socialized with their neighbors including the Riffles. Their daughter Mary Polly Van Scoyk was born in Fleming County, Kentucky, on September 27, 1796. Her sister, Sarah Van Scoyk married Jacob's brother Solomon.

Mary Polly died in 1853 at age fifty-seven in Darke County. Jacob and Mary Polly had eleven children including their third born, Aaron. The children were Mary Jane (1813); David (1816); Aaron (1817); Solomon (1818); Rachel (1820); Elizabeth (1822); Mariah (1826); Silas (1828); Elvina (1831); and Chauncey (1837).

Aaron Riffle was born in 1820, the year his grandfather David Riffle died. He was named after his other grandfather, Aaron Van Scoyk. On August 19, 1841, Aaron Riffle married Catherine Brown, a daughter of Mary White and George Brown, early settlers in Darke County. Nothing more is known of Catherine's father's parents, but Mary was the daughter of Joseph H. Wight, who was born in 1777 in New York and died before 1855 in Darke County. Reverend Wight married Sarah in 1796 presumably in New York.

Mary White was born in 1777 in New York and died after 1850 in Darke County. The Whites came to Brown Township in 1837. *The History of Darke County* mentions preaching was done in the home of White, near Dallas, now Ansonia. Their daughter Mary was born in 1799 and died in 1865. These dates are written in the Family Bible pages. Joseph Wight's (White) will mentions daughter Mary who married George R Brown, born in 1797. George and Mary were parents of Catherine Brown, wife of Aaron Riffle. George R Brown may have been related to Philip Brown who died intestate in 1848 leaving a widow Catherine. George R. had died in 1841 and is not mentioned in the court hearing in 1848.

The grandson of the frontiersman, David Riffle, Aaron Riffle was born July 19, 1820, as recorded in the Brown family Bible. He was the third of ten children born to Jacob and Mary Polly Riffle. Presumably, Aaron received little education in the rural schools of Darke County, Ohio. He no doubt helped his father Jacob on the farm while growing up. When he was twenty one he married Catherine Brown on August 19, 1841. She was seventeen. They farmed their land while raising six children: Fulton in 1841; Silas 1844; Mary Maretta 1845; George in 1847; Jacob in 1858; and John 1860. It is probable that Catherine had several stillbirths or infant deaths between George and Jacob's births.

An unforeseen event touched their lives and affected their children, an event that changed the course of American history, the Civil War. In 1861, the conflict began and soon interrupted the lives of many people. Two of Aaron and Catherine's sons enlisted in the service of the Union. Aaron, now age forty-one, most likely never imagined that he personally would play a part in this war as well. The war dragged on for three years. Their son Fulton enlisted in the Ohio Cavalry and Silas in the Ohio Volunteer Infantry. Fulton was captured in Louisville and eventually paroled. Aaron did not see his two sons come home nor did he learn that his future son-in-law, Beverly Marcum, would return only to succumb to lung disease in 1867.

The war continued for three years, and the Union army was forced to furlough enlistees at the termination of three years of service. Consequently, the Union instituted the draft in 1863. This act, the first in this country, embittered much of the public. New York City was the site of draft riots at that time. Unfortunately, the burden fell on those men with no resources. Those draftees with cash resources were able to buy the services of men who served, often temporarily, in their steads. It is estimated that very few of the men drafted actually served in what was considered an unbalanced and unfair system. Draft notices went out in March, May, and July of 1864.

Sometime in March of 1864, Aaron Riffle received his draft notice and orders to report to Camp Chase, Columbus, Ohio, by May 11, 1864. Aaron was forty-four, well beyond the age of the older draftees. There seems to be no record of why he was drafted at such an advanced age for military service. He evidently had no resources to buy a substitute or fight the system. Perhaps he felt compelled to serve because two of his sons and other relatives had enlisted. In any event, he joined the army and left wife Catherine and four children still at home to survive as best they could under less than desirable circumstances.

After a short period, Aaron was sent by rail to Virginia to join the Army of the Potomac commanded by General George Meade under the supreme commander General U.S. Grant. Aaron reported to the 122nd Ohio Volunteer Infantry, Third Division, VI Army Corps. During the time Aaron was making his way to join his regiment, the 122nd was taking part in the assault on the Salient, the "Bloody Angle" as it was called. The draftees had no knowledge of the part the VI Corps would play during the following year. Later, there must have been many times these men wondered why they were plucked from their normal lives in order to participate in some of the bloodiest and most horrific battles during the last year of the Civil War.

Aaron probably did not report to the 122 OVI until late in May, 1864. At that time the unit was on the right of the Union line on the North Anna River. Then began the Battle of Cold Harbor, the latter of which was simply a tavern at a crossroads in the backwoods of Virginia. The Battle of Cold Harbor began June 1, 1864, and lasted until the 12th of June. According to Bruce Catton in his book **Stillness of Appomattox**, the VI Corps held the right of the Union lines when Sheridan moved them to Cold Harbor. Catton relates,

The men remembered this march as about the worst they ever made. When they got to Cold Harbor in midmorning on June 1, they were dirt-caked and completely worn out" (151).Wright's VI Corps had marched for at least nine continuous hours for the second day in a row. The VI Corps had marched for longer periods than had any other corps or unit in either army.

One of the Union soldiers at Cold Harbor, James Bowen of the 37th Massachusetts relates as follows:

Then the march was taken up and steadily pursued, and seldom had the brave men struggled through a more server ordeal. The day proved intensely hot, the sun burning down with a lurid, brassy glare that seemed to broil the human flesh on which it fell; the

way led through sandy plains, heated to the intensity of a vast furnace, from which the most terrible clouds of dust arose not only high into the air, disclosing every movement to the watchful enemy, but as well choking the breath and blinding the vision of the gasping men who were marching through them. Everywhere the sun stroke did its deadly work - men fell blinded and gasping from the ranks, strong, brave men who on a dozen deadly fields had looked death in the face without quailing, conquered now by the long, unceasing strain to which they had been subject and the might power of the elements."

In early July 6, 1864, the 122 OVI was ordered to Baltimore, Maryland. They covered the Union retreat July 9 at Monocacy, Virginia. From August 7 until November 29 they participated in Sheridan's Shenandoah Campaign. By December 6, 1864, the 122 OVI was at the siege of Petersburg in Virginia. On April 2, 1865, they participated in the assault and consequent fall of Petersburg. The VI Corps and Sheridan's cavalry pursued Lee to Sailor's Creek and eventually Appomattox Court House. Sheridan and Grant were finally closing in.

According to Catton in *Stillness of Appomattox* "the VI Corps which had marched all day and night without food{because} Sheridan wanted help. . . veterans followed" (370). Catton also relates "the VI Corps marched through Appomattox on its way to the north side of the river..{and} saw General Grant on the porch. . . waved and yelled. . . marched to music. . . " (373). The war was over on Palm Sunday, April 9[th,] and Aaron and his regiment witnessed the conclusion. How sick Aaron and others were at this time is not known. Conditions, however, of the army camps, lack of medical knowledge, and the universal complaint of diarrhea took their toll. It is probably that Aaron was suffering as were others at this time. This forty-four year old man had spent a year with men half his age, fighting in horrible battles, sleeping on the ground, spending hours marching under extreme conditions of heat and cold, eating spoiled food, and drinking contaminated water. According to the Civil War Home Page, 995 out of 1000 men eventually contracted diarrhea.

Aaron Riffle's thoughts must have often been on his Darke County family and the fate of his wife and children. His misery must have been severe and constant. If he wrote Catherine, his wife, no letters survive today. Catherine must have felt similar agony wondering if her husband would return or if she could keep things together. The VI Corps marched to Danville April 17 and stayed there until May 16 when they were moved to Richmond, then to Washington D. C. from May 24 until June 1, 1865. The Corps Review was June 9, 1865, and the unit mustered out June 26. The regiment lost 7 officers and 86 enlisted men killed and mortally wounded and 137 men by diseases.

Aaron Riffle was unable to go home. He was hospitalized at that time. His pension report shows that he was in Augur Hospital, a hospital with 668 beds under surgeon G L Sutton. There were three other hospitals, most much larger. In any event, Aaron Riffle was stricken with severe diarrhea at the very least and never recovered. He spent at least the last month of his life, perhaps more, in a hospital bed slowly dying, never to return home. He was forty four. Aaron Riffle was dead by July

20, 1865, in an Alexandria army hospital of diarrhea and bilious fever. How often he must have wondered why a father of six children, in his forties, was taken from his farm and thrown into a war he probably never dreamed of. He may not have known the fate of his two sons who had enlisted in the service of the Union.

Aaron's records show that he was buried in Arlington National Cemetery. In 1865 only the poor or unidentified were buried there. The first soldier was buried in May 1864. At the end of the war 16,000 graves lined space next to Arlington House, the former property of Robert E Lee, ceded to the government in 1865 for $150,000. The first Memorial Day was announced from its portico in 1868.

The Adjunct General's Office granted Catherine Riffle a pension on May 24, 1866. Aaron was listed as having died July 20, 1865, of chronic diarrhea. On October 25, 1866, at age forty two, Catherine appeared in court to apply for an increase in her $8 per month pension. The petition was signed by Chauncey and Silas Riffle, brothers of her deceased husband Aaron. Catherine and children were in Brown Township and used Ansonia (Dallas) as their post office. Catherine did not live many years after her husband's death. She died in May of 1872 leaving two minor children who were adopted by their uncle David Riffle. She could not keep the farm, and her life must have been difficult because there was little income, forcing her to live on the charity of her Riffle brothers-in-law and uncles.

Of Catherine's four adult children, Mary Marietta was the third, born in 1845. Two of her brothers fought in the Civil War but lived to return to Darke County and raise large families. Family tradition suggests that one of these brothers was imprisoned at Louisville, Kentucky, and walked home after the war.

Mary Marietta's anguish did not end with her father's death. She married Civil War veteran Beverly Marcum in 1867. Within a little over a year he, too, died as a result of the war and left her with a three month old son Delius Larue Marcum. Needing help financially, she married Aaron Marker in Ansonia in 1870 and had another son, Everett Marker, in 1871. By 1874, Aaron had left her to support two sons on her own. It is not clear why the Markers divorced but both of Mary Marietta's marriages were of short duration. Life was extremely difficult for her and her young sons.

David and Margaret Riffle's children left many descendants, some of whom remain in Darke County, Ohio, and others who are scattered throughout the country.

Epilogue

The author descends from all four families described in this work. Obviously, there are many more tales of family members that are not known or included here. All of the families produced Revolutionary War and Civil War soldiers, many of whom lost their lives while serving this country. It is interesting that all four families had participants at the Battle of Point Pleasant in 1774, sometimes called the first battle of the Revolution.

Today, throughout the country, there are perhaps tens of thousands of descendants of these enterprising Germans, most of whom do not know of their heritage. Perhaps this narrative will encourage descendants to become interested in their ancestry and the remarkable people who settled this country.

www.ingramcontent.com/pod-product-compliance
Lightning Source LLC
Chambersburg PA
CBHW050359290526
45786CB00003B/1046